THE POETRY BOOK—4

nd his eyes are kind —

THE POETRY BOOK

MIRIAM BLANTON HUBER

HERBERT B. BRUNER
and
CHARLES MADISON CURRY

Illustrated by
MARJORIE HARTWELL

Granger Poetry Library

GRANGER BOOK CO., INC.
Great Neck, N.Y.

First Published 1926
Reprinted 1979

International Standard Book Number
0-89609-183-X

Library of Congress Catalog Number
79-51968

Printed in the United States of America

THE CONTENTS

[v]

THE POETRY BOOK—4

BOOK HOUSES

I always think the cover of
   A book is like a door
Which opens into some one's house
   Where I've not been before.

A pirate or a fairy queen
   May lift the latch for me;
I always wonder, when I knock,
   What welcome there will be.

And when I find a house that's dull
   I do not often stay,
But when I find one full of friends
   I'm apt to spend the day.

I never know what sort of folks
   Will be within, you see,
And that's why reading always is
   So int'resting to me.

       — ANNIE FELLOWS JOHNSTON

THE HEIGHT OF THE RIDICULOUS

I wrote some lines once on a time,
  In wondrous merry mood,
And thought, as usual, men would say
  They were exceeding good.

They were so queer, so very queer,
  I laughed as I would die;
Albeit, in the general way,
  A sober man am I.

I called my servant, and he came;
  How kind it was of him
To mind a slender man like me,
  He of the mighty limb.

"These to the printer," I exclaimed,
  And, in my humorous way,
I added (as a trifling jest),
  "There'll be the devil to pay."

He took the paper, and I watched,
  And saw him peep within;
At the first line he read, his face
  Was all upon the grin.

He read the next; the grin grew broad,
   And shot from ear to ear;
He read the third; a chuckling noise
   I now began to hear.

The fourth; he broke into a roar;
   The fifth; his waistband split;
The sixth; he burst five buttons off,
   And tumbled in a fit.

Ten days and nights, with sleepless eye,
   I watched that wretched man,
And since, I never dare to write
   As funny as I can.

           — OLIVER WENDELL HOLMES

A STRANGE WILD SONG

He thought he saw a Buffalo
    Upon the chimney-piece:
He looked again, and found it was
    His Sister's Husband's Niece.
"Unless you leave this house," he said,
    "I'll send for the Police."

He thought he saw a Rattlesnake
    That questioned him in Greek:
He looked again, and found it was
    The Middle of Next Week.
"The one thing I regret," he said,
    "Is that it cannot speak!"

He thought he saw a Banker's Clerk
    Descending from the 'bus:
He looked again, and found it was
    A Hippopotamus.
"If this should stay to dine," he said,
    "There won't be much for us!"

He thought he saw a Kangaroo
    That worked a coffee-mill;
He looked again, and found it was
    A Vegetable-Pill.
"Were I to swallow this," he said,
    "I should be very ill."

He thought he saw a Coach and Four
    That stood beside his bed:
He looked again, and found it was
    A Bear without a Head.
"Poor thing," he said, "poor silly thing!
    It's waiting to be fed!"

He thought he saw an Albatross
    That fluttered round the Lamp:
He looked again, and found it was
    A Penny Postage-Stamp.
"You'd best be getting home," he said:
    "The nights are very damp!"

He thought he saw a Garden Door
    That opened with a key:
He looked again, and found it was
    A Double-Rule-of-Three:
"And all its mystery," he said,
    "Is clear as day to me!"

He thought he saw an Argument
    That proved he was the Pope:
He looked again, and found it was
    A Bar of Mottled Soap.
"A fact so dread," he faintly said,
    "Extinguishes all hope!"

                    — Lewis Carroll

MR. NOBODY

I know a funny little man,
    As quiet as a mouse,
Who does the mischief that is done
    In everybody's house!

There's no one ever sees his face,
    And yet we all agree
That every plate we break was cracked
    By Mr. Nobody.

'Tis he who always tears our books,
    Who leaves the door ajar,
He pulls the buttons from our shirts,
    And scatters pins afar;

That squeaking door will always squeak,
    For, prithee, don't you see,
We leave the oiling to be done
    By Mr. Nobody.

He puts damp wood upon the fire,
    That kettles cannot boil;
His are the feet that bring in mud,
    And all the carpets soil.

The finger marks upon the door
    By none of us are made;

We never leave the blinds unclosed,
    To let the curtains fade.

The ink we never spill; the boots
    That lying round you see
Are not our boots;— they all belong
    To Mr. Nobody.

— AUTHOR UNKNOWN

MORNING

Will there really be a morning?
    Is there such a thing as day?
Could I see it from the mountains
    If I were as tall as they?

Has it feet like water-lilies?
    Has it feathers like a bird?
Is it brought from famous countries
    Of which I have never heard?

Oh, some scholar!   Oh, some sailor!
    Oh, some wise man from the skies!
Please to tell a little pilgrim
    Where the place called morning lies!

— EMILY DICKINSON

THE QUEST

There once was a restless boy
  Who dwelt in a home by the sea,
Where the water danced for joy
  And the wind was glad and free:
But he said, "Good mother, oh! let me go;
For the dullest place in the world, I know,
  Is this little brown house,
  This old brown house,
    Under the apple tree.

"I will travel east and west;
  The loveliest homes I'll see;
And when I have found the best,
  Dear mother, I'll come for thee.
I'll come for thee in a year and a day,
And joyfully then we'll haste away
  From this little brown house,
  This old brown house,
    Under the apple tree."

So he traveled here and there,
  But never content was he,
Though he saw in lands most fair
  The costliest homes there be.
He something missed from the sea or sky,
Till he turned again, with a wistful sigh,

To the little brown house,
The old brown house,
    Under the apple tree.

Then the mother saw and smiled,
    While her heart grew glad and free.
"Hast thou chosen a home, my child?
    Ah, where shall we dwell?" quoth she.
And he said, "Sweet mother, from east to west,
The loveliest home, and the dearest and best,
    Is a little brown house,
    An old brown house,
        Under an apple tree."

— Eudora S. Bumstead

WHAT TO LOOK FOR

Do not look for wrong and evil—
    You will find them if you do;
As you measure for your neighbor
    He will measure back to you.

Look for goodness, look for gladness,
    You will meet them all the while;
If you bring a smiling visage
    To the glass, you meet a smile.

— Alice Cary

MY DOG

I have no dog, but it must be
Somewhere there's one belongs to me—
A little chap with wagging tail,
And dark brown eyes that never quail,
But look you through, and through, and through
With love unspeakable, but true.

Somewhere it must be, I opine,
There is a little dog of mine
With cold black nose that sniffs around
In search of what things may be found
In pocket, or some nook hard by
Where I have hid them from his eye.

Somewhere my doggie pulls and tugs
The fringes of rebellious rugs,
Or with the mischief of the pup
Chews all my shoes and slippers up,
And when he's done it to the core
With eyes all eager pleads for more.

Somewhere upon his hinder legs
My little doggie sits and begs,
And in a wistful minor tone
Pleads for the pleasures of the bone—
I pray it be his owner's whim
To yield, and grant the same to him.

Somewhere a little dog doth wait,
It may be by some garden-gate,
With eyes alert and tail attent—
You know the kind of tail that's meant—
With stores of yelps of glad delight
To bid me welcome home at night.

Somewhere a little dog is seen,
His nose two shaggy paws between,
Flat on his stomach, one eye shut
Held fast in dreamy slumber, but
The other open, ready for
His master coming through the door.

— JOHN KENDRICK BANGS

JUMILHAC-THE-GRAND

Oh, the baron was French, he was very French,
  And he lived in France, did he,
In a castle set on a hill alone,
A beauteous seven-towered castle of stone,
  That was just as French as he.

Seven beauteous firm round towers it had,
  A tower for each daughter fair,
With many windows, a pointed roof,
  And a winding turret stair.

And lo, when the seventh tower was built,
  The castle front was filled;
And wasn't he proud of the handsome sight
And didn't he dance and prance in delight
  And weren't the neighbors thrilled?

Now, it came to pass one day in spring
  That the baron had a son;
The baron smiled, but he wrung his hands,
  Whatever could be done!

Oh, the baron was glad to have his son,
  He had wanted him right along;
But where could he possibly build him a tower,
Oh, where could he build him a firm round tower
  That would not look all wrong!

He called his architects, one, two, three,
   And his pipers, four, five, six,
And they stood and pondered and beat their heads,
   It was a frightful fix!

Then cried the one with the longest beard,
   "He is but a little chap,
He's a bit of a boy in a rounded hood,
And a round-topped tower for him we could
   Tuck into the castle's lap."

And at Jumilhac there's the castle still,
   With a round-capped tower that is wee,
And seven towers that are tall and firm,
   And as French as French can be.

—EMMA L. BROCK

THE CIRCUS-DAY PARADE

Oh! the Circus-Day parade! How the bugles played
    and played!
And how the glossy horses tossed their flossy manes
    and neighed,
As the rattle and the rhyme of the tenor-drummer's
    time
Filled all the hungry hearts of us with melody sublime!

How the grand band-wagon shone with a splendor all
    its own,
And glittered with a glory that our dreams had never
    known!
And how the boys behind, high and low of every
    kind,
Marched in unconscious capture, with a rapture
    undefined!

How the horsemen, two and two, with their plumes of
    white and blue
And crimson, gold and purple, nodding by at me and
    you,
Waved the banners that they bore, as the Knights in
    days of yore,
Till our glad eyes gleamed and glistened like the
    spangles that they wore!

And, last of all, the Clown,
making mirth for all the town

How the graceless-graceful stride of the elephant was
  eyed,
And the capers of the little horse that cantered at his
  side!
How the shambling camels, tame to the plaudits of
  their fame,
With listless eyes came silent, masticating as they came.

How the cages jolted past, with each wagon battened fast,
And the mystery within it only hinted of at last
From the little grated square in the rear, and nosing
  there
The snout of some strange animal that sniffed the
  outer air!

And, last of all, The Clown, making mirth for all the town,
With his lips curved ever upward and his eyebrows
  ever down,
And his chief attention paid to the little mule that
  played
A tattoo on the dashboard with his heels, in the parade.

Oh! The Circus-Day parade! How the bugles played
  and played!
And how the glossy horses tossed their flossy manes
  and neighed,
As the rattle and the rhyme of the tenor-drummer's time
Filled all the hungry hearts of us with melody sublime!

— James Whitcomb Riley

QUEEN MAB

A little fairy comes at night,
    Her eyes are blue, her hair is brown,
With silver spots upon her wings,
    And from the moon she flutters down.

She has a little silver wand,
    And when a good child goes to bed
She waves her hand from right to left,
    And makes a circle round its head.

And then it dreams of pleasant things,
    And fountains filled with fairy fish,
And trees that bear delicious fruit,
    And bow their branches at a wish:

Of arbors filled with dainty scents
    From lovely flowers that never fade;
Bright flies that glitter in the sun,
    And glow-worms shining in the shade.

And talking birds with gifted tongues,
    For singing songs and telling tales,
And pretty dwarfs to show the way
    Through fairy hills and fairy dales.

But when a bad child goes to bed,
    From left to right she weaves her rings,

And then it dreams all through the night
   Of only ugly horrid things!

Then lions come with glaring eyes,
   And tigers growl, a dreadful noise,
And ogres draw their cruel knives,
   To shed the blood of girls and boys.

Then stormy waves rush on to drown,
   Or raging flames come scorching round,
Fierce dragons hover in the air,
   And serpents crawl along the ground.

Then wicked children wake and weep,
   And wish the long black gloom away;
But good ones love the dark, and find
   The night as pleasant as the day.

                   — THOMAS HOOD

BARBARA FRIETCHIE

Up from the meadows rich with corn,
Clear in the cool September morn,

The clustered spires of Frederick stand
Green-walled by the hills of Maryland.

Round about them orchards sweep,
Apple and peach tree fruited deep,

Fair as the garden of the Lord
To the eyes of the famished rebel horde,

On that pleasant morn of the early fall
When Lee marched over the mountain-wall;

Over the mountains winding down,
Horse and foot, into Frederick town.

Forty flags with their silver stars,
Forty flags with their crimson bars,

Flapped in the morning wind: the sun
Of noon looked down, and saw not one.

Up rose old Barbara Frietchie then,
Bowed with her four score years and ten;

Bravest of all in Frederick town,
She took up the flag the men hauled down;

In her attic window the staff she set,
To show that one heart was loyal yet.

Up the street came the rebel tread,
Stonewall Jackson riding ahead.

Under his slouched hat left and right
He glanced; the old flag met his sight.

"Halt!" — the dust-brown ranks stood fast.
"Fire!" — out blazed the rifle-blast.

It shivered the window, pane and sash;
It rent the banner with seam and gash.

Quick as it fell, from the broken staff
Dame Barbara snatched the silken scarf.

She leaned far out on the window-sill,
And shook it forth with a royal will.

"Shoot, if you must, this old gray head,
But spare your country's flag," she said.

A shade of sadness, a blush of shame,
Over the face of the leader came;

The nobler nature within him stirred
To life at that woman's deed and word;

"Who touches a hair of yon gray head
Dies like a dog!   March on!" he said.

All day long through Frederick street
Sounded the tread of marching feet.

All day long that free flag tost
Over the heads of the rebel host.

Ever its torn folds rose and fell
On the loyal winds that loved it well;

And through the hill-gaps sunset light
Shone over it with a warm good-night.

Barbara Frietchie's work is o'er,
And the Rebel rides on his raids no more.

Honor to her! and let a tear
Fall, for her sake, on Stonewall's bier.

Over Barbara Frietchie's grave,
Flag of Freedom and Union, wave!

Peace and order and beauty draw
Round thy symbol of light and law;

And ever the stars above look down
On thy stars below in Frederick town!

— JOHN GREENLEAF WHITTIER

FAIRY MEN

Have you ever heard the tapping of the fairy cobbler
    men,
When the moon is shining brightly thro' the branches
    in the glen?
Have you seen a crew of goblins in a water-lily boat,
Softly sliding, gently gliding,
'Mid the rushes tall afloat?

Have you seen the sleeping goblins 'neath the mush-
    rooms on the hills?
Have you heard the rippling music of the tiny fairy rills?
Have you seen the looms where spiders spin their
    sparkling silver threads?
Brightly shining and entwining
Round the nodding flower heads?

Have you seen the magic circles where the little fairies
    play,
From the last soft flush of sunset, till the first bright
    gleam of day?
Have you seen a band of fairies, with their pickaxes
    so bold,
Talking gravely, trudging bravely,
Off to seek for fairy gold?

If you want to see the fairies, you must visit them at
    night,
When the silvery stars are gleaming and the moon is
    shining bright.
If you make no sound to warn them, you will see the
    fairy men
Laughing, singing, harebells ringing,
While the moonbeams light the glen.

—SYBIL MORFORD

A PROVERB

A soft answer turneth away wrath;
But grievous words stir up anger.

—THE BIBLE

THE STRANGE MAN

His face was the oddest that ever was seen,
His mouth stood across 'twixt his nose and his chin;
Whenever he spoke it was then with his voice,
And in talking he always made some sort of noise.
                    Derry down.

He'd an arm on each side to work when he pleased,
But he never worked hard when he lived at his ease;
Two legs he had got to make him complete,
And what is more odd, at each end were his feet.

His legs, as folks say, he could move at his will,
And when he was walking he never stood still.
If you were to see him, you'd laugh till you burst,
For one leg or the other would always be first.

If this whimsical fellow had a river to cross,
If he could not get over, he staid where he was,
He seldom or ever got off the dry ground,
So great was his luck that he never was drowned.

But the reason he died and the cause of his death
Was owing, poor soul, to the want of more breath;
And now he is left in the grave for to moulder,
Had he lived a day longer, he'd have been a day older.
                    Derry down.

                              — Author Unknown

A MAN OF WORDS

A man of words and not of deeds
Is like a garden full of weeds;
And when the weeds begin to grow,
It's like a garden full of snow;
And when the snow begins to fall,
It's like a bird upon the wall;
And when the bird away does fly,
It's like an eagle in the sky;
And when the sky begins to roar,
It's like a lion at the door;
And when the door begins to crack,
It's like a stick across your back;
And when your back begins to smart,
It's like a penknife in your heart;
And when your heart begins to bleed,
You're dead, and dead, and dead, indeed.

— Old Folk Rhyme

THE FAIRIES

Up the airy mountain,
  Down the rushy glen,
We daren't go a-hunting
  For fear of little men;
Wee folk, good folk,
  Trooping all together;
Green jacket, red cap,
  And white owl's feather!

Down along the rocky shore
  Some make their home;
They live on crispy pancakes
  Of yellow tide-foam;
Some in the reeds
  Of the black mountain-lake,
With frogs for their watch-dogs,
  All night awake.

High on the hilltop
  The old King sits;
He is now so old and gray
  He's nigh lost his wits.
With a bridge of white mist
  Columbkill he crosses,
On his stately journeys
  From Slieveleague to Rosses;

Wee folk, good folk,
Trooping all together;

Or going up with music
  On cold starry nights,
To sup with the Queen
  Of the gay Northern Lights.

They stole little Bridget
  For seven years long;
When she came down again
  Her friends were all gone.
They took her lightly back
  Between the night and morrow;
They thought that she was fast asleep,
  But she was dead with sorrow.
They have kept her ever since
  Deep within the lake,
On a bed of flag-leaves,
  Watching till she wake.

By the craggy hillside,
  Through the mosses bare,
They have planted thorn-trees
  For pleasure here and there.
Is any man so daring
  As dig them up in spite,
He shall find their sharpest thorns
  In his bed at night.

Up the airy mountain,
   Down the rushy glen,
We daren't go a-hunting
   For fear of little men;
Wee folk, good folk,
   Trooping all together;
Green jacket, red cap,
   And white owl's feather!

—William Allingham

GLIMPSE IN AUTUMN

Ladies at a ball
   Are not so fine as these
   Richly brocaded trees
That decorate the fall.

They stand against a wall
   Of crisp October sky,
   Their plumed heads held high,
Like ladies at a ball.

—Jean Starr Untermeyer

THERE WAS A LITTLE GIRL

There was a little girl, and she had a little curl,
  Right down the middle of her forehead,
When she was good, she was very, very good,
  But when she was bad, she was horrid.

One day she went upstairs, while her parents, unawares,
  In the kitchen down below were occupied with meals,
And she stood upon her head, on her little truckle-bed,
  And she then began hurraying with her heels.

Her mother heard the noise, and thought it was the
    boys,
  A-playing at a combat in the attic,
But when she climbed the stair and saw Jemima there,
  She took and she did whip her most emphatic!

                    — AUTHOR UNKNOWN

THE MIST AND ALL

I like the fall,
The mist and all.
I like the night owl's
Lonely call—
And wailing sound
Of wind around.

I like the gray
November day,
And bare, dead boughs
That coldly sway
Against my pane.
I like the rain.

I like to sit
And laugh at it—
And tend
My cozy fire a bit.
I like the fall—
The mist and all.—

— DIXIE WILLSON

THE OLD WOMAN OF THE ROADS

Oh, to have a little house!
To own the hearth and stool and all!
The heaped-up sods upon the fire,
The pile of turf against the wall!

To have a clock with weights and chains,
And pendulum swinging up and down!
A dresser filled with shining delf,
Speckled with white and blue and brown!

I could be busy all the day
Cleaning and sweeping hearth and floor,
And fixing on their shelf again
My white and blue and speckled store!

I could be quiet there at night
Beside the fire, and by myself,
Sure of a bed and loth to leave
The ticking clock and shining delf!

Och! but I'm weary of mist and dark,
And roads where there's never a house or bush,
And tired I am of bog and road,
And the crying wind and the lonesome hush!

And I'm praying to God on high,
And I'm praying Him night and day,
For a little house — a house of my own, —
Out of the wind's and rain's way.

— PADRAIC COLUM

From *Wild Earth and Other Poems*, by Padraic Colum.   Reprinted by special arrangement with The Macmillan Company, publishers.

THE LAND OF NOD

From breakfast on through all the day
At home among my friends I stay,
But every night I go abroad
Afar into the land of Nod.

All by myself I have to go,
With none to tell me what to do—
All alone beside the streams
And up the mountain sides of dreams.

The strangest things are there for me,
Both things to eat and things to see,
And many frightening sights abroad,
Till morning in the land of Nod.

Try as I like to find the way,
I never can get back by day,
Nor can remember plain and clear
The curious music that I hear.

—Robert Louis Stevenson

NONSENSE VERSES

I

There was an Old Man with a beard
Who said, "It is just what I feared!
    Two Owls and a Hen,
    Four Larks and a Wren,
Have all built their nests in my beard!"

II

There was an Old Man who said, "How
Shall I flee from this horrible Cow?
    I will sit on this stile
    And continue to smile,
Which may soften the heart of that cow!"

III

There was an Old Man in a boat,
Who said, "I'm afloat!   I'm afloat!"
    When they said, "No, you ain't!"
    He was ready to faint,
That unhappy Old Man in a boat.

— EDWARD LEAR

ROMANCE

I saw a ship a-sailing,
  A-sailing on the sea;
Her masts were of the shining gold,
  Her deck of ivory;
And sails of silk, as soft as milk,
  And silvern shrouds had she.

And round about her sailing,
  The sea was sparkling white,
The waves all clapped their hands and sang
  To see so fair a sight.
They kissed her twice, they kissed her thrice,
  And murmured with delight.

Then came the gallant captain,
  And stood upon the deck;
In velvet coat, and ruffles white,
  Without a spot or speck;
And diamond rings, and triple strings
  Of pearls around his neck.

And four-and-twenty sailors
  Were round him bowing low;
On every jacket three times three
  Gold buttons in a row;
And cutlasses down to their knees;
  They made a goodly show.

And then the ship went sailing,
 A-sailing o'er the sea;
She dived beyond the setting sun,
 But never back came she,
For she found the lands of the golden sands,
 Where the pearls and diamonds be.

— GABRIEL SETOUN

A TRAGIC STORY

There lived a sage in days of yore,
And he a handsome pigtail wore;
But wondered much and sorrowed more
   Because it hung behind him.

He mused upon this curious case,
And swore he'd change the pigtail's place,
And have it hanging at his face,
   Not dangling there behind him.

Said he, "The mystery I've found,—
I'll turn me round,"—he turned him round;
   But still it hung behind him.

Then round and round, and out and in,
All day the puzzled sage did spin;
In vain—it mattered not a pin—
   The pigtail hung behind him.

And right, and left, and round about,
And up, and down, and in, and out,
He turned; but still the pigtail stout
   Hung steadily behind him.

And though his efforts never slack,
And though he twist, and twirl, and tack,
Alas! still faithful to his back,
   The pigtail hangs behind him.

           — WILLIAM MAKEPEACE THACKERAY

A THANKSGIVING FABLE

It was a hungry pussy cat,
  Upon Thanksgiving morn,
And she watched a thankful little mouse
  That ate an ear of corn.

"If I ate that thankful little mouse,
  How thankful he should be,
When he has made a meal himself
  To make a meal for me!

"Then with his thanks for having fed,
  And his thanks for feeding me,
With all *his* thankfulness inside,
  How thankful I shall be!"

Thus "mewsed" the hungry pussy cat,
  Upon Thanksgiving Day;
But the little mouse had overheard
  And declined (with thanks) to stay.

— Oliver Herford

A GOOD THANKSGIVING

Said old Gentleman Gay, "On a Thanksgiving Day,
If you want a good time, then give something away."
So he sent a fat turkey to Shoemaker Price,
And the shoemaker said, "What a big bird! how nice!
And, since a good dinner's before me, I ought
To give poor Widow Lee the small chicken I bought."

"This fine chicken, Oh, see!" said the pleased Widow
    Lee,
"And the kindness that sent it, how precious to me!
I would like to make someone as happy as I —
I'll give Washwoman Biddy my big pumpkin pie."

"And Oh, sure!" Biddy said, " 'Tis the queen of all pies!
Just to look at its yellow face gladdens my eyes!
Now it's my turn, I think, and a sweet ginger-cake
For the motherless Finigan children I'll bake."

"A sweet cake, all our own! 'Tis too good to be true!"
Said the Finigan children, Rose, Denny, and Hugh;
"It smells sweet of spice, and we'll carry a slice
To poor little lame Jake, who has nothing that's nice."

"Oh, I thank you, and thank you!" said little lame Jake,
"Oh, what a beautiful, beautiful, beautiful cake!

And Oh, such a big slice! I will save all the crumbs,
And will give 'em to each little sparrow that comes!"

And the sparrows they twittered, as if they would say,
Like old Gentleman Gay, "On a Thanksgiving Day,
If you want a good time, then give something away."

—Marian Douglas

AMERICA THE BEAUTIFUL

O beautiful for spacious skies,
  For amber waves of grain,
For purple mountain majesties
  Above the fruited plain!
    America! America!
  God shed His grace on thee
And crown thy good with brotherhood
  From sea to shining sea!

O beautiful for pilgrim feet,
  Whose stern, impassioned stress
A thoroughfare for freedom beat
  Across the wilderness!
    America! America!
  God mend thine every flaw,
Confirm thy soul in self-control,
  Thy liberty in law!

O beautiful for heroes proved
  In liberating strife,
Who more than self their country loved,
  And mercy more than life!
    America! America!
  May God thy gold refine,
Till all success be nobleness,
    And every gain divine!

O beautiful for patriot dream
  That sees beyond the years
Thine alabaster cities gleam
  Undimmed by human tears!
    America! America!
  God shed His grace on thee
And crown thy good with brotherhood
  From sea to shining sea!

      —KATHARINE LEE BATES

FOUR THINGS

Four things a man must learn to do
If he would make his record true:
To think without confusion clearly;
To love his fellow men sincerely;
To act from honest motives purely;
To trust in God and Heaven securely.

      —HENRY VAN DYKE

THE ORGAN GRINDER

Just an organ grinder;
Grind, grind, grind.
Silly monkey on his shoulder,
But his face is kind,
So kind.
Down the street he shuffles,
Children march behind.
Silly monkey making faces,
Grind, grind, grind.
Little wheezy organ,
Tired as his feet;
Harmony all broken,
But the tune is sweet.
Just an organ grinder,
Grinding at our gate;
Wait, wait, wait,
But his heart is great.
Grind, grind, grind.
And his eyes are kind—
Soft and kind,
Good and kind.

—John Martin

SUPPOSE

Suppose, my little lady,
 Your doll should break her head,
Could you make it whole by crying
 Till your eyes and nose are red?
And wouldn't it be pleasanter
 To treat it as a joke;
And say you're glad 'twas dolly's
 And not your head that broke?

Suppose you're dressed for walking,
 And the rain comes pouring down,
Will it clear off any sooner
 Because you scold and frown?
And wouldn't it be better
 For you to smile than pout,
And so make sunshine in the house,
 When there is none without?

Suppose your task, my little man,
 Is very hard to get,
Will it make it any easier
 For you to sit and fret?
And wouldn't it be wiser
 Than waiting like a dunce,
To go to work in earnest
 And learn the thing at once?

Suppose the world doesn't please you,
  Nor the way some people do,
Do you think the whole creation
  Will be altered just for you?
And isn't it, my boy or girl,
  The wisest, bravest plan,
Whatever comes or doesn't come,
  To do the best you can?

—Phoebe Cary

PROVERBS

There be four things which are little upon
  the earth,
But they are exceeding wise:

The ants are a people not strong,
Yet they prepare their meat in the summer;

The conies[1] are but a feeble folk,
Yet they make their houses in the rocks;

The locusts have no king,
Yet they go forth all of them by bands;

The spider taketh hold with her hands,
And is in kings' palaces.

—The Bible

1 Conies are thought to be little animals like rabbits.

THE TABLE AND THE CHAIR

Said the Table to the Chair,
"You can hardly be aware
How I suffer from the heat
And from chilblains on my feet.
If we took a little walk,
We might have a little talk;
Pray let us take the air,"
Said the Table to the Chair.

Said the Chair unto the Table,
"Now, you *know* we are not able:
How foolishly you talk,
When you know we *cannot* walk!"
Said the Table with a sigh,
"It can do no harm to try.
I've as many legs as you:
Why can't we walk on two?"

So they both went slowly down,
And walked about the town
With a cheerful bumpy sound
As they toddled round and round;
And everybody cried,
As they hastened to their side,
"See! the Table and the Chair
Have come out to take the air!"

"See! the Table and the Chair
Have come out to take the air!"

But in going down an alley
To a castle in a valley,
They completely lost their way,
And wandered all the day;
Till, to see them safely back,
They paid a Ducky-quack,
And a Beetle, and a Mouse,
Who took them to their house.

Then they whispered to each other,
"O delightful little brother,
What a lovely walk we've taken!
Let us dine on beans and bacon."
So the Ducky and the leetle
Browny-Mousy and the Beetle
Dined, and danced upon their heads
Till they toddled to their beds.

— EDWARD LEAR

THE WIND AND THE MOON

Said the Wind to the Moon, "I will blow you out;
   You stare
   In the air
  Like a ghost in a chair,
Always looking what I am about;
I hate to be watched; I will blow you out."

The Wind blew hard, and out went the Moon.
   So, deep
   On a heap
  Of clouds to sleep,
Down lay the Wind, and slumbered soon —
Muttering low, "I've done for that Moon."

He turned in his bed; she was there again!
   On high,
   In the sky,
  With her one ghost eye,
The Moon shone white and alive and plain.
Said the Wind — "I will blow you out again."

The Wind blew hard, and the Moon grew dim.
   "With my sledge
   And my wedge
  I have knocked off her edge!
If only I blow right fierce and grim,
The creature will soon be dimmer than dim."

He blew and he blew, and she thinned to a thread.
        "One puff
        More's enough
      To blow her to snuff!
One good puff more where the last was bred,
And glimmer, glimmer, glum will go that thread!"

He blew a great blast and the thread was gone.
        In the air
        Nowhere
      Was a moonbeam bare;
Far-off and harmless the shy stars shone;
Sure and certain the Moon was gone!

The Wind he took to his revels once more;
        On down,
        In town,
      Like a merry-mad clown,
He leaped and halloed with·whistle and roar,—
"What's that?" The glimmering thread once more!

He flew in a rage—he danced and blew;
        But in vain
        Was the pain
      Of his bursting brain;
For still the broader the Moon-scrap grew
The broader he swelled his big cheeks and blew.

Slowly she grew — till she filled the night,
        And shone
        On her throne
    In the sky alone,
A matchless, wonderful, silvery light,
Radiant and lovely, the Queen of the night.

Said the Wind, "What a marvel of power am I!
        With my breath,
        Good faith,
    I blew her to death —
First blew her away right out of the sky —
Then blew her in; what a strength am I!"

But the Moon she knew nothing about the affair;
        For high
        In the sky,
    With her one white eye,
Motionless, miles above the air,
She had never heard the great Wind blare.

—George Macdonald

THE RUNAWAY

Once, when the snow of the year was beginning to fall,
We stopped by a mountain pasture to say "Whose
colt?"
A little Morgan had one forefoot on the wall,
The other curled at his breast.   He dipped his head
And snorted to us.   And then he had to bolt.
We heard the miniature thunder where he fled
And we saw him or thought we saw him dim and gray,
Like a shadow against the curtain of falling flakes.
"I think the little fellow's afraid of the snow.
He isn't winter-broken.   It isn't play
With the little fellow at all.   He's running away.
I doubt if even his mother could tell him, 'Sakes,
It's only weather.'   He'd think she didn't know.
Where is his mother?   He can't be out alone."
And now he comes again with a clatter of stone
And mounts the wall again with whited eyes
And all his tail that isn't hair up straight.
He shudders his coat as if to throw off flies.
"Whoever it is that leaves him out so late,
When other creatures have gone to stall and bin,
Ought to be told to come and take him in."

— ROBERT FROST

HOW THEY BROUGHT THE GOOD NEWS FROM GHENT TO AIX

I sprang to the stirrup, and Joris, and he;
I galloped, Dirck galloped, we galloped all three;
"Good speed!" cried the watch, as the gatebolts
undrew;
"Speed!" echoed the wall to us galloping through;
Behind shut the postern, the lights sank to rest,
And into the midnight we galloped abreast.

Not a word to each other; we kept the great pace
Neck by neck, stride by stride, never changing our
place;
I turned in my saddle and made its girths tight,
Then shortened each stirrup, and set the pique right,
Rebuckled the cheek strap, chained slacker the bit,
Nor galloped less steadily Roland a whit.

'Twas moonset at starting; but while we drew near
Lokeren, the cocks crew and twilight dawned clear;
At Boom, a great yellow star came out to see;
At Düffeld, 'twas morning as plain as could be;
And from Mecheln church steeple we heard the half-
chime,
So Joris broke silence with, "Yet there is time!"

At Aershot, up leaped of a sudden the sun,
And against him the cattle stood black every one,

To stare through the mist at us galloping past,
And I saw my stout galloper Roland at last,
With resolute shoulders, each butting away
The haze, as some bluff river headland its spray:

And his low head and crest, just one sharp ear bent
    back
For my voice, and the other pricked out on his track;
And one eye's black intelligence,—ever that glance
O'er its white edge at me, his own master, askance!
And the thick heavy spume-flakes which aye and anon
His fierce lips shook upwards in galloping on.

By Hasselt, Dirck groaned; and cried Joris, "Stay
    spur!
Your Roos galloped bravely, the fault's not in her,
We'll remember at Aix"—for one heard the quick
    wheeze
Of her chest, saw the stretched neck and staggering
    knees,
And sunk tail, and horrible heave of the flank,
As down on her haunches she shuddered and sank.

So, we were left galloping, Joris and I,
Past Looz and past Tongres, no cloud in the sky;
The broad sun above laughed a pitiless laugh,
'Neath our feet broke the brittle bright stubble like
    chaff;

Till over by Dalhem a dome spire sprang white,
And "Gallop," gasped Joris, "for Aix is in sight!"

"How they'll greet us!"—and all in a moment his
  roan
Rolled neck and croup over, lay dead as a stone;
And there was my Roland to bear the whole weight
Of the news which alone could save Aix from her fate,
With his nostrils like pits full of blood to the brim,
And with circles of red for his eye sockets' rim.

Then I cast loose my buffcoat, each holster let fall,
Shook off both my jack boots, let go belt and all,
Stood up in the stirrup, leaned, patted his ear,
Called my Roland his pet name, my horse without peer;
Clapped my hands, laughed and sang, any noise, bad
  or good,
Till at length into Aix Roland galloped and stood.

And all I remember is—friends flocking round
As I sat with his head 'twixt my knees on the ground;
And no voice but was praising this Roland of mine,
As I poured down his throat our last measure of wine,
Which (the burgesses voted by common consent)
Was no more than his due who brought good news
  from Ghent.

—ROBERT BROWNING

BEAUTIFUL MEALS

How nice it is to eat!
All creatures love it so,
That they who first did spread,
Ere breaking bread,
A cloth like level snow,
Were right, I know.

And they were wise and sweet
Who, glad that meats taste good,
Used speech in an arch style,
And oft would smile
To raise the cheerful mood,
While at their food.

And those who first, so neat,
Placed fork and knife quite straight,
The glass on the right hand;
And all, as planned,
Each day set round the plate,—
Be their praise great!

For then, their hearts being light,
They plucked hedge-posies bright—
Flowers who, their scent being sweet,
Give nose and eye a treat:

'Twas they, my heart can tell,
Not eating fast but well,
Who wove the spell
Which finds me every day,
And makes each meal-time gay;
I know 'twas they.

—T. Sturge Moore

WINDY NIGHTS

Whenever the moon and stars are set,
  Whenever the wind is high,
All night long in the dark and wet,
  A man goes riding by.
Late in the night when the fires are out,
Why does he gallop and gallop about?

Whenever the trees are crying aloud,
  And the ships are tossed at sea,
By, on the highway, low and loud,
  By at the gallop goes he.
By at the gallop he goes, and then
By he comes back at the gallop again.

—Robert Louis Stevenson

CHRISTMAS EVERYWHERE

Everywhere, everywhere, Christmas to-night!
Christmas in lands of the fir-tree and pine,
Christmas in lands of the palm-tree and vine,
Christmas where snow peaks stand solemn and white,
Christmas where cornfields lie sunny and bright.

Christmas where children are hopeful and gay,
Christmas where old men are patient and gray,
Christmas where peace, like a dove in his flight,
Broods o'er brave men in the thick of the fight;
Everywhere, everywhere, Christmas to-night!

For the Christ-child who comes is the master of all;
No palace too great, and no cottage too small.

— PHILLIPS BROOKS

By permission from *Christmas Songs and Easter Carols* by Phillips Brooks. Copyright by E. P. Dutton & Company.

WHEN AT CHRISTMAS CHRIST WAS BORN
(XVI Century)

When at Christmas Christ was born,
   In far Palestine,
All observed that solemn day
   With a joy divine.
There was neither churl nor King
Who did not a present bring,
And who offered ever with their best endeavor.

There was one who gave a lamb
   With his heart and soul,
And another brought some milk
   In a little bowl.
One beneath his smock, 'tis said,
Brought a humble gift of bread
For the Mother holy, and for Joseph lowly.

There was not a single wight
   But he came to see:
Even from far Moorish lands
   Journeyed monarchs three.
The poor princes from the East,
Came with prayers that never ceased,
The incense, myrrh, and gold which all admire.

—Old Carol

MARCH OF THE THREE KINGS

This highway
Beheld at break of day
Three Eastern Kings go by upon their journey.
This highway
Beheld at break of day
Three Eastern Kings go by in rich array.
With courage high
All their guards passed by,
Their knights-at-arms with the squires and the pages.
With courage high
All their guards passed by,
With gilded armor shining like the sky.

Wondering then,
I watched the mighty men,
I stood amazed as the knights were passing.
Wondering then,
I watched the mighty men,
And as they passed I followed them again.
They journeyed far
To the guiding star
That shone where Jesus was lying in a manger.
And far away
Where the Christ Child lay
They found the shepherds come to watch and pray.

Gaspard old
Had brought a gift of gold.
He said, "My Lord, Thou art the King of Glory."
Gaspard old
Gave Christ his gift of gold,
And that this Child would conquer death, he told.
Then incense sweet
At the Christ Child's feet
King Melchior placed, saying, "Thou art God of
armies.
Although He lies
Here in humble guise,
This little Child is God of earth and skies."

"You will die;
For You, my Lord, I cry,"
Wept Balthazar, his gifts of myrrh presenting.
"You will die
And in a tomb will lie,
For on a cross you will be lifted high."
All we to-day
To the Child must pray,
Who came to earth with His gifts of peace and blessing,
To Him we pray
And our homage pay
And with the Kings we march along the way.

—Old Provençal Carol

A FAREWELL

My fairest child, I have no song to give you;
   No lark could pipe to skies so dull and gray:
Yet, ere we part, one lesson I can leave you
     For every day.

Be good, sweet maid, and let who will be clever;
   Do noble things, not dream them, all day long;
And so make life, death, and that vast forever
     One grand, sweet song.

              — CHARLES KINGSLEY

GOOD NAME

Good name in man and woman, dear my lord,
Is the immediate jewel of their souls:
Who steals my purse steals trash; 'tis something,
    nothing;
'Twas mine, 'tis his, and has been slave to thousands;
But he that filches from me my good name
Robs me of that which not enriches him,
And makes me poor indeed.

              — WILLIAM SHAKESPEARE

THE GARDEN YEAR

January brings the snow,
Makes our feet and fingers glow.

February brings the rain,
Thaws the frozen lake again.

March brings breezes, loud and shrill,
To stir the dancing daffodil.

April brings the primrose sweet,
Scatters daisies at our feet.

May brings flocks of pretty lambs
Skipping by their fleecy dams.

June brings tulips, lilies, roses,
Fills the children's hands with posies.

Hot July brings cooling showers,
Apricots, and gillyflowers.

August brings the sheaves of corn,
Then the harvest home is borne.

Warm September brings the fruit;
Sportsmen then begin to shoot.

Fresh October brings the pheasant;
Then to gather nuts is pleasant.

Dull November brings the blast;
Then the leaves are whirling fast.

Chill December brings the sleet,
Blazing fire, and Christmas treat.

—Sara Coleridge

THE FLIGHT

A pipe and a spoon and a tenpenny nail,
Stole a tin dishpan and went for a sail.
But the cook he grew curious,
Fussy, and furious;
Gathered his trappings, and went on their trail.
He found them that night in a pitiful plight,
And sent them all home on the ten o'clock mail.

—Leroy F. Jackson

WHAT THE WINDS BRING

Which is the wind that brings the cold?
  The North Wind, Freddie; and all the snow,
And the sheep will scamper into the fold,
  When the North begins to blow.

Which is the wind that brings the heat?
  The South Wind, Katy; and corn will grow,
And peaches redden for you to eat,
  When the South begins to blow.

Which is the wind that brings the rain?
  The East Wind, Arty; and farmers know
That cows come shivering up the lane,
  When the East begins to blow.

Which is the wind that brings the flowers?
  The West Wind, Bessy; and soft and low
The birdies sing in the summer hours,
  When the West begins to blow.

— EDMUND CLARENCE STEDMAN

STOPPING BY WOODS ON A SNOWY EVENING

Whose woods these are I think I know.
His house is in the village though;
He will not see me stopping here
To watch his woods fill up with snow.

My little horse must think it queer
To stop without a farmhouse near
Between the woods and frozen lake
The darkest evening of the year.

He gives his harness bells a shake
To ask if there is some mistake.
The only other sound's the sweep
Of easy wind and downy flake.

The woods are lovely, dark, and deep.
But I have promises to keep,
And miles to go before I sleep,
And miles to go before I sleep.

— ROBERT FROST

HOW TO TELL THE WILD ANIMALS

If ever you should go by chance
To jungles in the East;
And if there should to you advance
A large and tawny beast,
If he roars at you as you're dyin'
You'll know it is the Asian Lion.

Or if some time when roaming round,
A noble wild beast greets you,
With black strips on a yellow ground,
Just notice if he eats you.
This simple rule may help you learn
The Bengal Tiger to discern.

If strolling forth, a beast you view,
Whose hide with spots is peppered,
As soon as he has lept on you,
You'll know it is the leopard.
'Twill do no good to roar with pain,
He'll only lep and lep again.

If when you're walking round your yard,
You meet a creature there,
Who hugs you very, very hard,
Be sure it is the Bear.
If you have any doubt, I guess
He'll give you just one more caress.

Though to distinguish beasts of prey
A novice might nonplus,
The Crocodiles you always may
Tell from Hyenas thus:
Hyenas come with merry smiles;
But if they weep, they're Crocodiles.

The true Chameleon is small,
A lizard sort of thing;
He hasn't any ears at all,
And not a single wing.
If there is nothing on the tree,
'Tis the Chameleon you see.

—CAROLYN WELLS

DON'T GIVE UP

If you've tried and have not won,
    Never stop for crying;
All that's good and great is done
    Just by patient trying.

Though young birds, in flying, fall,
    Still their wings grow stronger;
And the next time they can keep
    Up a little longer.

Though the sturdy oak has known
    Many a wind that bowed her,
She has risen again and grown
    Loftier and prouder.

If by easy work you beat,
    Who the more will prize you?
Gaining victory from defeat,
    That's the test that tries you.

— PHOEBE CARY

THE BLIND MEN AND THE ELEPHANT

It was six men of Indostan,
    To learning much inclined,
Who went to see the Elephant
    (Though all of them were blind),
That each by observation
    Might satisfy his mind.

The *First* approached the Elephant,
    And happening to fall
Against his broad and sturdy side,
    At once began to bawl:
"God bless me! but the Elephant
    Is very like a wall!"

The *Second*, feeling of the tusk,
    Cried, "Ho! what have we here
So very round and smooth and sharp?
    To me 'tis mighty clear
This wonder of an Elephant
    Is very like a spear!"

The *Third* approached the animal,
    And happening to take
The squirming trunk within his hands,
    Thus boldly up and spake:
"I see," quoth he, "the Elephant
    Is very like a snake!"

And so these men of Indostan
Disputed loud and long

The *Fourth* reached out his eager hand,
   And felt about the knee.
"What most this wondrous beast is like,
   Is mighty plain," quoth he;
" 'Tis clear enough the Elephant
   Is very like a tree!"

The *Fifth*, who chanced to touch the ear,
   Said: "E'en the blindest man
Can tell what this resembles most;
   Deny the fact who can,
This marvel of an Elephant
   Is very like a fan!"

The *Sixth* no sooner had begun
   About the beast to grope,
Than, seizing on the swinging tail
   That fell within his scope,
"I see," quoth he, "the Elephant
   Is very like a rope!"

And so these men of Indostan
   Disputed loud and long,
Each in his own opinion
   Exceeding stiff and strong,
Though each was partly in the right,
   And all were in the wrong!

— JOHN GODFREY SAXE

O CAPTAIN! MY CAPTAIN!

O Captain! my Captain! our fearful trip is done,
The ship has weather'd every rack, the prize we sought
is won,
The port is near, the bells I hear, the people all exulting,
While follow eyes the steady keel, the vessel grim and
daring;
But O heart! heart! heart!
O the bleeding drops of red,
Where on the deck my Captain lies,
Fallen cold and dead.

O Captain! my Captain! rise up and hear the bells;
Rise up—for you the flag is flung—for you the bugle
trills,
For you bouquets and ribbon'd wreaths—for you the
shores a-crowding,
For you they call, the swaying mass, their eager faces
turning;
Here Captain, dear father!
This arm beneath your head!
It is some dream that on the deck,
You've fallen cold and dead.

My Captain does not answer, his lips are pale and still,
My father does not feel my arm, he has no pulse nor
will,

The ship is anchor'd safe and sound, its voyage closed
and done,
From fearful trip the victor ship comes in with object
won;
Exult, O shores! and ring, O bells!
But I with mournful tread,
Walk the deck my Captain lies,
Fallen cold and dead.

— WALT WHITMAN

DO YOU FEAR THE WIND?

Do you fear the force of the wind,
The slash of the rain?
Go face them and fight them,
Be savage again.
Go hungry and cold like the wolf,
Go wade like the crane:
The palms of your hands will thicken,
The skin of your cheek will tan;
You'll grow ragged and weary and swarthy,
But you'll walk like a man!

— HAMLIN GARLAND

THE SHADOW PEOPLE

Old lame Bridget doesn't hear
Fairy music in the grass
When the gloaming's on the mere
And the shadow people pass;
Never hears their slow, grey feet
Coming from the village street
Just beyond the parson's wall,
Where the clover globes are sweet
And the mushroom's parasol
Opens in the moonlit rain.
Every night I hear them call
From their long and merry train,
Old lame Bridget says to me,
"It is just your fancy, child."
She cannot believe I see
Laughing faces in the wild,
Hands that twinkle in the sedge
Where the finny minnows quiver,
Shaping on a blue wave's ledge
Bubble foam to sail the river.
And the sunny hands to me
Beckon ever, beckon ever.
Oh! I would be wild and free
And with the shadow people be.

—Francis Ledwidge

WHAT SPOILED THE POT PIE

A SAILOR'S YARN

I. Well—one time down in *Gastinal*
      We tied up near the jetty
      Right near a crowd of *Gandizans*
      A-dancing in the scrub;
   And a-boiling on a fire
      That was roaring like a furnace
      Was a big, black kettle going
      BLUB—BLUB—BLUB !

II. The Captain called the carpenter
      And gave him word to hurry;
      He sent him to the after deck
      To rig him up a seat.
   Said the captain, "These black savages
      Are cooking something smelly;
      Now it is not cabbage and it—
      IS—NOT—MEAT!"

III.. The boatswain sent me up the shrouds
      To rig a fall and tackle.
      I climbed clear to the skysail yard
      And hitched a pulley fast,
   While the natives they were yelling
      And the smell grew so much stronger
      That it set me coughing as it
      PASSED—THE—MAST.

IV. The carpenter came running up,
    And everybody hurried.
    The captain took his spyglass
    And we swayed him up aloft.
  We could see him as he swung there,
    A-looking and a-looking,
    Then he yelled and signaled to us—
    THEN—*HE*—COUGHED.

 V. And when the Captain reached the deck
    He said, "DASH IN MY TIMBERS!
    Those savages are crazy as
    A double-headed snake!
  The trouble all was started,
    As near as I can make it
    When the chief's wife
    PUT HIS RUBBERS—
        IN THE KETTLE—
        BY MISTAKE!"—

—WALT HARRIS

THE YEAR'S AT THE SPRING

The year's at the spring
And day's at the morn;
Morning's at seven;
The hillside's dew-pearled;
The lark's on the wing;
The snail's on the thorn:
God's in his heaven—
All's right with the world!

—ROBERT BROWNING

SEVEN HATEFUL THINGS

Proverbs 6: 16–19

These six things doth the Lord hate: yea, seven are
an abomination unto him:
A proud look,
A lying tongue,
And hands that shed innocent blood,
A heart that deviseth wicked imaginations,
Feet that be swift in running to mischief,
A false witness that speaketh lies,
And he that soweth discord among brethren.

—THE BIBLE

MY HEART'S IN THE HIGHLANDS

My heart's in the Highlands, my heart is not here;
My heart's in the Highlands a-chasing the deer;
Chasing the wild deer and following the roe,
My heart's in the Highlands wherever I go.
Farewell to the Highlands, farewell to the North,
The birthplace of valor, the country of worth;
Wherever I wander, wherever I rove,
The hills of the Highlands forever I love.

Farewell to the mountains high covered with snow,
Farewell to the straths and green valleys below,
Farewell to the forests and wild-hanging woods,
Farewell to the torrents and loud-pouring floods.
My heart's in the Highlands, my heart is not here,
My heart's in the Highlands a-chasing the deer;
Chasing the wild deer and following the roe,
My heart's in the Highlands wherever I go.

— ROBERT BURNS

THE RAIN SONG

It isn't raining rain to me,
   It's raining daffodils;
In every dimpled drop I see
   Wild flowers on the hills;
The clouds of gray engulf the day
   And overwhelm the town;
It isn't raining rain to me,
   It's raining roses down.

It isn't raining rain to me,
   But fields of clover bloom,
Where every buccaneering bee
   May find a bed and room;
A health unto the happy!
   A fig for him who frets!
It isn't raining rain to me,
   It's raining violets.

— ROBERT LOVEMAN.

THE COMING OF SPRING

There's something in the air
That's new and sweet and rare —
A scent of summer things,
A whir as if of wings.

There's something, too, that's new
In the color of the blue
That's in the morning sky,
Before the sun is high.

And though on plain and hill
'Tis winter, winter still,
There's something seems to say
That winter's had its day.

And all this changing tint,
This whispering stir and hint
Of bud and bloom and wing,
Is the coming of the spring.

And tomorrow or today
The brooks will break away
From their icy, frozen sleep,
And run, and laugh, and leap.

And the next thing, in the woods,
The catkins in their hoods

Of fur and silk will stand,
A sturdy little band.

And the tassels soft and fine
Of the hazel will entwine,
And the elder branches show
Their buds against the snow.

So, silently but swift,
Above the wintry drift,
The long days gain and gain,
Until on hill and plain, —

Once more, and yet once more,
Returning as before,
We see the bloom of birth
Make young again the earth.

— NORA PERRY

THE SONG-SPARROW

There is a bird I know so well,
    It seems as if he must have sung
    Beside my crib when I was young;
Before I knew the way to spell
    The name of even the smallest bird,
    His gentle-joyful song I heard.
Now see if you can tell, my dear,
What bird it is that, every year,
Sings "*Sweet — sweet — sweet — very merry cheer.*"

He comes in March, when winds are strong,
    And snow returns to hide the earth;
    But still he warms his heart with mirth,
And waits for May.   He lingers long
    While flowers fade; and every day
    Repeats his small, contented lay;
As if to say, we need not fear
The season's change, if love is here
With "*Sweet — sweet — sweet — very merry cheer.*"

He does not wear a Joseph's-coat
    Of many colors, smart and gay;
    His suit is Quaker brown and gray,
With darker patches at his throat.
    And yet of all the well-dressed throng
    No one can sing so brave a song.

It makes the pride of looks appear
A vain and foolish thing, to hear
His "*Sweet — sweet — sweet — very merry cheer.*"

A lofty place he does not love,
    But sits by choice, and well at ease,
    In hedges, and in little trees
That stretch their slender arms above
    The meadow-brook; and there he sings
    Till all the field with pleasure rings;
And so he tells in every ear,
That lowly homes to heaven are near
In "*Sweet — sweet — sweet — very merry cheer.*"

I like the tune, I like the words;
    They seem so true, so free from art,
    So friendly, and so full of heart,
That if but one of all the birds
    Could be my comrade everywhere,
    My little brother of the air,
I'd choose the song-sparrow, my dear,
Because he'd bless me, every year,
With "*Sweet — sweet — sweet — very merry cheer.*"

— HENRY VAN DYKE

THE TWINS

In form and feature, face and limb,
   I grew so like my brother,
That folks got taking me for him,
   And each for one another.
It puzzled all our kith and kin,
   It reached an awful pitch;
For one of us was born a twin,
   Yet not a soul knew which.

One day (to make the matter worse),
   Before our names were fixed,
As we were being wash'd by nurse
   We got completely mixed;
And thus, you see, by Fate's decree,
   (Or rather nurse's whim),
My brother John got christened me,
   And I got christened him.

This fatal likeness even dogg'd
   My footsteps when at school,
And I was always getting flogg'd,
   For John turned out a fool.
I put this question hopelessly
   To every one I knew—
What would you do, if you were me,
   To prove that you were you?

Our close resemblance turned the tide
 Of my domestic life;
For somehow my intended bride
 Became my brother's wife.
In short, year after year the same
 Absurd mistakes went on;
And when I died—the neighbors came
 And buried brother John!

—Henry S. Leigh

AN APPLE ORCHARD IN THE SPRING

Have you seen an apple orchard in the spring?
  In the spring?
An English apple orchard in the spring?
When the spreading trees are hoary,
With their wealth of promised glory,
And the mavis sings its story
  In the spring?

Have you plucked the apple blossoms in the spring?
  In the spring?
And caught their subtle odors in the spring?
Picked buds bursting at the light,
Crumpled petals baby-white,
Just to touch them a delight —
  In the spring?

Have you walked beneath the blossoms in the spring?
  In the spring?
Beneath the apple blossoms in the spring?
When the pink cascades are falling,
And the silver brooklets brawling,
And the cuckoo bird soft calling,
  In the spring?
If you have not, then you know not, in the spring,
  In the spring,
Half the color, beauty, wonder of the spring.

No such sight can I remember,
Half so precious, half so tender,
As the apple blossoms render,
      In the spring.

          — WILLIAM MARTIN

A COMPARISON

Apple blossoms look like snow,
They're different, though.
Snow falls softly, but it brings
Noisy things:
Sleighs and bells, forts and fights,
Cosy nights.
But apple blossoms when they go,
White and slow,
Quiet all the orchard space,
Till the place
Hushed with falling sweetness seems
Filled with dreams.

          —JOHN FARRAR

WE THANK THEE

For mother-love and father-care,
For brothers strong and sisters fair,
For love at home and here each day,
For guidance lest we go astray,
    Father in Heaven, we thank thee.

For this new morning with its light,
For rest and shelter of the night,
For health and food, for love and friends,
For ev'rything His goodness sends,
    Father in Heaven, we thank Thee.

For flowers that bloom about our feet,
For tender grass, so fresh, so sweet,
For song of bird and hum of bee,
For all things fair we hear or see,
    Father in Heaven, we thank Thee.

For blue of stream and blue of sky,
For pleasant shade of branches high,
For fragrant air and cooling breeze,
For beauty of the blooming trees,
    Father in Heaven, we thank Thee.

—Author Unknown

THE HENS

The night was coming very fast
It reached the gate as I ran past.

The pigeons had gone to the tower of the church,
And all the hens were on their perch

Up in the barn, and I thought I heard
A piece of a little purring word.

I stopped inside, waiting and staying,
To try to hear what the hens were saying.

They were asking something, that was plain,
Asking it over and over again.

One of them moved and turned around,
Her feathers made a ruffled sound,

A ruffled sound, like a bushful of birds,
And she said her little asking words.

She pushed her head close into her wing,
But nothing answered anything.

— Elizabeth Madox Roberts

They were asking something, that was plain,

APPLE-SEED JOHN

Poor Johnny was bended well nigh double
With years of toil, and care, and trouble;
But his large old heart still felt the need
Of doing for others some kindly deed.

"But what can I do?" old Johnny said:
"I who work so hard for daily bread?
It takes heaps of money to do much good;
I am far too poor to do as I would."

The old man sat thinking deeply a while,
Then over his features gleamed a smile,
And he clapped his hands with boyish glee,
And said to himself: "There's a way for me!"

He worked, and he worked with might and main,
But no one knew the plan in his brain.
He took ripe apples in pay for his chores,
And carefully cut from them all the cores.

He filled a bag full, then wandered away,
And no man saw him for many a day.
With knapsack over his shoulder slung,
He marched along, and whistled or sung.

He seemed to roam with no object in view,
Like one who had nothing on earth to do;
But, journeying thus o'er the prairies wide,
He paused now and then, and his bag untied.

With pointed cane deep holes he would bore,
And in every hole he placed a core;
Then covered them well, and left them there
In keeping of sunshine, rain, and air.

Sometimes for days he waded through grass,
And saw not a living creature pass,
But often, when sinking to sleep in the dark,
He heard the owls hoot and the prairie dogs bark.

Sometimes an Indian of sturdy limb
Came striding along and walked with him;
And he who had food shared with the other,
As if he had met a hungry brother.

When the Indian saw how the bag was filled,
And looked at the holes that the white man drilled,
He thought to himself 'twas a silly plan
To be planting seed for some future man.

Sometimes a log cabin came in view,
Where Johnny was sure to find jobs to do,
By which he gained stores of bread and meat,
And rest for his weary feet.

He had full many a story to tell,
And goodly hymns that he sung right well;
He tossed up the babes, and joined the boys
In many a game of fun and noise.

And he seemed so hearty, in work or play,
Men, women, and boys all urged him to stay;
But he always said: "I have something to do,
And I must go on to carry it through."

The boys, who were sure to follow him round,
Soon found what it was he put in the ground;
And so, as time passed and he traveled on,
Ev'ry one called him "Old Apple-Seed John."

Whenever he'd used the whole of his store,
He went into cities and worked for more;
Then he marched back to the wilds again,
And planted seed on hillside and plain.

In cities, some said the old man was crazy;
While others said he was only lazy;
But he took no notice of gibes and jeers,
He knew he was working for future years.

He knew that trees would soon abound
Where once a tree could not have been found;
That a flick'ring play of light and shade
Would dance and glimmer along the glade;

That blossoming sprays would form fair bowers,
And sprinkle the grass with rosy showers;
And the little seeds his hands had spread,
Would become ripe apples when he was dead.

So he kept on traveling far and wide,
Till his old limbs failed him, and he died.
He said at the last: " 'Tis a comfort to feel
I've done good in the world, though not a
    great deal."

Weary travelers, journeying west,
In the shade of his trees find pleasant rest;
And they often start, with glad surprise,
At the rosy fruit that round them lies.

And if they inquire whence came such trees,
Where not a bough once swayed in the breeze,
The answer still comes, as they travel on:
"These trees were planted by Apple-Seed John."

—LYDIA MARIA CHILD

SLEEPIN' OUT

Once let a feller git in tune
  With all outdoors, there hain't no use
Fer him to think he kin ferget,
  Or from the wild's big ways jar loose.
He's always thinkin' 'bout them nights—
  Jes' listen now, and hear him sigh,
A-dreamin' of an old tarp bed,
  And sleepin' out beneath the sky.

There hain't no bunk in any house,
  That to the warm earth kin compare;
She's sort o' kind and comfortin',
  And gives you strength as you lie there.
And then, besides, you gulp all night
  The clean, sweet air; and in the morn
There hain't a doubt or fear but what
  Your rested soul jes' laughs to scorn.

—Robert V. Carr

THE BRONC THAT WOULDN'T BUST

I've busted bronchos off and on
Since first I struck their trail,
And you bet I savvy bronchos
From nostrils down to tail;
But I struck one on Powder River,
And say, hands, he was the first
And only living broncho
That your servant couldn't burst.

He was a no-count buckskin,
Warn't worth two-bits to keep,
Had a black stripe down his backbone,
And was woolly like a sheep.
That hoss warn't built to tread the earth:
He took natural to the air:
And every time he went aloft
He tried to leave me there.

He went so high above the earth
Lights from Jerusalem shone.
Right thar we parted company
And he came down alone.
I hit terra firma,
The buckskin's heels struck free
And brought a bunch of stars along
To dance in front of me.

I'm not a-riding airships
Nor an electric flying beast:
Ain't got no rich relation
A-waitin' me back East:
So I'll sell my chaps and saddle,
My spurs can lay and rust;
For there's now and then a digger
That a buster cannot bust.

— AUTHOR UNKNOWN

A TWISTER

A thatcher of Thatchwood went to Thatchet a-thatch-
ing.
Did a thatcher of Thatchwood go to Thatchet a-thatch-
ing?
If a thatcher of Thatchwood went to Thatchet a-thatch-
ing,
Where's the thatching the thatcher of Thatchwood
has thatched?

— OLD NONSENSE

OLD SUSAN

When Susan's work was done she'd sit,
With one fat guttering candle lit,
And window opened wide to win
The sweet night air to enter in;
There, with a thumb to keep her place,
She'd read, with stern and wrinkled face,
Her mild eyes gliding very slow
Across the letters to and fro,
While wagged the guttering candle flame
In the wind that through the window came.

And sometimes in the silence she
Would mumble a sentence audibly,
Or shake her head as if to say,
"You silly souls, to act this way!"
And never a sound from night I'd hear,
Unless some far-off cock crowed clear;
Or her old shuffling thumb should turn
Another page; and rapt and stern,
Through her great glasses bent on me
She'd glance into reality;
And shake her round old silvery head,·
With—"You!—I thought you was in bed!"—
Only to tilt her book again,
And rooted in Romance remain.

—WALTER DE LA MARE

THE LEPRACAUN
OR
FAIRY SHOEMAKER

Little Cowboy, what have you heard,
　Up on the lonely rath's green mound?
Only the plaintive yellow bird
　Sighing in sultry fields around,
Chary, chary, chary, chee-ee!—
Only the grasshopper and the bee?—
　　"Tip-tap, rip-rap,
　　Tick-a-tack-too!
Scarlet leather, sewn together,
　This will make a shoe.
　Left, right, pull it tight;
　　Summer days are warm;
　Underground in winter,
　　Laughing at the storm!"
Lay your ear close to the hill.
Do you not catch the tiny clamor,
Busy click of elfin hammer,
Voice of the Lepracaun singing shrill
　As he merrily plies his trade?
　　He's a span
　　And a quarter in height.
　Get him in sight, hold him tight,
　　And you're a made
　　　Man!

You watch your cattle the summer day,
Sup on potatoes, sleep in the hay;
    How would you like to roll in your carriage,
    Look for a duchess's daughter in marriage?
Seize the Shoemaker—then you may!
        "Big boots a-hunting,
        Sandals in the hall,
    White for a wedding-feast,
        Pink for a ball.
    This way, that way,
        So we make a shoe;
    Getting rich every stitch,
        Tick-tack-too!"
Nine-and-ninety treasure-crocks
This keen miser-fairy hath,
Hid in mountains, woods and rocks,
Ruin and round-tower, cave and rath,
    And where the cormorants build;
        From time of old
        Guarded by him;
        Each of them filled
        Full to the brim
            With gold!

I caught him at work one day, myself
    In the castle-ditch, where foxglove grows, —
A wrinkled, wizened, and bearded Elf,

Spectacles stuck on his pointed nose,
Silver buckles to his hose,
Leather apron—shoe in his lap—
   "Rip-rap, tip-tap,
   Tack-tack-too!
(A grasshopper on my cap!
   Away the moth flew!)
Buskins for a fairy prince,
   Brogues for his son,—
Pay me well, pay me well,
   When the job is done!"
The rogue was mine, beyond a doubt.
I stared at him; he stared at me;
"Servant, Sir!" "Humph!" says he,
   And pull'd a snuff-box out.

He took a long pinch, looked better pleased,
   The queer little Lepracaun;
Offered the box with a whimsical grace,—
Pouf! he flung the dust in my face,
   And, while I sneezed,
      Was gone!

—William Allingham

THE CATERPILLAR

Under this loop of honeysuckle,
A creeping, colored caterpillar,
I gnaw the fresh green hawthorn spray,
I nibble it leaf by leaf away.

Down beneath grow dandelions,
Daisies, old-man's-looking-glasses;
Rooks fly croaking across the lane.
I eat and swallow and eat again.

Here come raindrops helter-skelter;
I munch and nibble unregarding:
Hawthorn leaves are juicy and firm.
I'll mind my business: I'm a good worm.

Under this loop of honeysuckle,
A hungry, hairy caterpillar,
I crawl on my high and swinging seat,
And eat, eat, eat—as one ought to eat.

— ROBERT GRAVES

SEVEN TIMES ONE

There's no dew left on the daisies and clover,
   There's no rain left in heaven;
I've said my "seven times" over and over,
   Seven times one are seven.

I am old, so old I can write a letter;
   My birthday lessons are done;
The lambs play always, they know no better;
   They are only one times one.

O moon! in the night I have seen you sailing
   And shining so round and low;
You were bright! ah, bright! but your light is failing,—
   You are nothing now but a bow.

You moon, have you done something wrong in heaven
   That God has hidden your face?
I hope if you have you will soon be forgiven
   And shine again in your place.

O velvet bee, you're a dusty fellow;
   You've powdered your legs with gold!
O brave marsh marybuds, rich and yellow,
   Give me your money to hold!

O columbine, open your folded wrapper,
   Where two twin turtledoves dwell!
O cuckoopint, toll me the purple clapper
   That hangs in your clear, green bell!

And show me your nest with the young ones in it,—
   I will not steal them away;
I am old! you may trust me, linnet, linnet,—
   I am seven times one to-day.

— JEAN INGELOW

THE SWALLOW'S NEST

Day after day her nest she moulded,
   Building with magic, love and mud,
A gray cup made by a thousand journeys,
   And the tiny beak was trowel and hod.

—EDWIN ARNOLD

THE BOY AND THE SHEEP

"Lazy sheep, pray tell me why
In the pleasant field you lie,
Eating grass and daisies white,
From the morning till the night.
Everything can something do,
But what kind of use are you?"

"Nay, my little master, nay;
Do not serve me so, I pray!
Don't you see the wool that grows
On my back, to make you clothes?
Cold, oh, very cold you'd be,
If you had no wool from me.

"True, it seems a pleasant thing,
To nip the daisies in the spring;
But many chilly nights I pass
On the cold and dewy grass,
Or pick a scanty dinner where
All the ground is brown and bare.

"Then the farmer comes at last,
When the merry spring is past,
And cuts my woolly fleece away,
For your coat in wintry day.
Little master, this is why
In the pleasant field I lie."

—Jane Taylor

THE LAMBKINS

What can lambkins do,
  All the keen night through?
Nestle by their woolly mother,
  The careful ewe.

What can nestlings do
  In the nightly dew?
Sleep beneath their mother's wing
  Till day breaks anew.

—Christina G. Rossetti

EVENING AT THE FARM

Over the hill the farm-boy goes.
His shadow lengthens along the land,
A giant staff in a giant hand;
In the poplar-tree, above the spring,
The katydid begins to sing;
   The early dews are falling;—
Into the stone-heap darts the mink;
The swallows skim the river's brink;
And home to the woodland fly the crows,
When over the hill the farm-boy goes,
Cheerily calling,
"Co', boss! co', boss! co'! co'! co'!"
Farther, farther, over the hill,
Faintly calling, calling still,
   "Co', boss! co', boss! co'! co'!"

Into the yard the farmer goes,
With grateful heart, at the close of day:
Harness and chain are hung away;
In the wagon-shed stand yoke and plow,
The straw's in the stack, the hay in the mow
   The cooling dews are falling;
The friendly sheep his welcome bleat,
The pigs come grunting to his feet
And the whinnying mare her master knows,

When into the yard the farmer goes,
  His cattle calling, —
   "Co', boss! co', boss! co'! co'! co'!"
While still the cow-boy, far away,
Goes seeking those that have gone astray, —
   "Co', boss! co', boss! co'! co'!"

Now to her task the milkmaid goes.
The cattle come crowding through the gate,
Lowing, pushing, little and great;
About the trough, by the farmyard pump,
The frolicsome yearlings frisk and jump,
  While the pleasant dews are falling; —
The new milch heifer is quick and shy,
But the old cow waits with tranquil eye,
And the white stream into the bright pail flows,
When to her task the milkmaid goes,
  Soothingly calling,
   "So, boss! so, boss! so! so! so!"

The cheerful milkmaid takes her stool,
And sits and milks in the twilight cool,
  Saying, "So! so, boss! so! so!"
To supper at last the farmer goes.
The apples are pared, the paper read,
The stories are told, then all to bed.
Without, the crickets' ceaseless song
Makes shrill the silence all night long;
  The heavy dews are falling.

The housewife's hand has turned the lock;
Drowsily ticks the kitchen clock;
The household sinks to deep repose,
But still in sleep the farm-boy goes
   Singing, calling,—
    "Co', boss! co', boss! co'! co'! co'!"
And oft the milkmaid, in her dreams,
Drums in the pail with the flashing streams,
   Murmuring "So, boss! so!"

— JOHN TOWNSEND TROWBRIDGE

THE ROSE

The lily has an air,
   And the snowdrop a grace,
And the sweet-pea a way,
   And the heart's-ease a face,—
Yet there's nothing like the rose
   When she blows.

—CHRISTINA G. ROSSETTI

LITTLE WHITE LILY

Little white Lily
Sat by a stone,
Drooping and waiting
Till the sun shone.
Little white Lily
Sunshine has fed;
Little white Lily
Is lifting her head.

Little white Lily
Said, "It is good—
Little white Lily's
Clothing and food."
Little white Lily
Dressed like a bride!
Shining with whiteness,
And crownèd beside!

Little white Lily
Droopeth with pain,
Waiting and waiting
For the wet rain.
Little white Lily
Holdeth her cup;
Rain is fast falling
And filling it up.

Little white Lily
Said, "Good again —
When I am thirsty
To have the nice rain!
Now I am stronger;
Now I am cool;
Heat cannot burn me,
My veins are so full."

Little white Lily
Smells very sweet:
On her head sunshine,
Rain at her feet.
"Thanks to the sunshine,
Thanks to the rain!
Little white Lily
Is happy again!"

—George Macdonald

NOBODY KNOWS

Winds of the morning,
Bending the grasses,
Drinking the dewdrops,
Kissing the rose,
Where do you go
When the meadows are quiet
And sleepy at noontime?
Nobody knows.

Winds of the evening,
That dance in the tree tops,
And sweep away clouds
From the moon till she glows,
Why don't you blow
Away the Old Sandman
That makes me so sleepy?
Nobody knows!

—HELEN COALE CREW

THE SEA MAID'S SONG

Though all my beads are truly pearls,
I'm really quite like other girls,
    Most anywhere.
Of course the sea is always wet
Where I like best to play,—and yet
    It looks like air.

Sometimes I even work for hours
At pulling seaweed from the flowers,—
    And then I sing,—
While ocean birds flock down to see
If they can be of help to me
    With anything.

The windy water blows my hair;
So, just to show I do not care,
    I toss my head.
But when at night the castle bell
Rings out, I have to mind it well—
    And go to bed.

—ANNE MOEN CLEELAND

Sometimes I even work for hours
At pulling seaweed from the flowers

KITTY CAUGHT A HORNET

Kitty caught a hornet,
Put it in a cage,
Fed it burs and buttermilk,
Got it in a rage;
Gave it lots of lettuce leaves,
Ice and smelling salts,
Whistled it a lively tune
And it began to waltz;
Gave it batting for a bed,
Snug and warm and deep,
Fanned it with a feather
And it went off to sleep.

—LEROY F. JACKSON

THE RIVULET

Run, little rivulet, run!
Summer is fairly begun.
Bear to the meadow the hymn of the pines,
And the echo that rings where the waterfall shines;
Run, little rivulet, run!

Run, little rivulet, run!
Sing of the flowers, every one:
Of the delicate harebell and violet blue;
Of the red mountain rosebud, all dripping with dew;
Run, little rivulet, run!

Run, little rivulet, run!
Carry the perfume you won
From the lily, that woke when the morning was gray,
To the white waiting moonbeam adrift on the bay;
Run, little rivulet, run!

Run, little rivulet, run!
Stay not till summer is done!
Carry the city the mountain birds' glee;
Carry the joy of the hills to the sea;
Run, little rivulet, run!

—Lucy Larcom

UP A HILL AND A HILL

Up a hill and a hill there's a sudden orchard slope,
   And a little tawny field in the sun,
There's a gray wall that coils like a twist of frayed-
    out rope,
   And grasses nodding news one to one.

Up a hill and a hill there's a windy place to stand,
   And between the apple-boughs to find the blue
Of the sleepy summer sea, past the cliffs of orange sand,
   And the white charmed ships sliding through.

Up a hill and a hill there's a little house as gray
   As a stone that the glaciers scored and stained;
With a red rose by the door, and a tangled garden way,
   And a face at the window, checker-paned.

I could climb, I could climb, till the shoes fell off my
    feet,
   Just to find that tawny field above the sea!
Up a hill and a hill, — oh, the honeysuckle's sweet!
   And the eyes at the window watch for me!

—Fannie Stearns Gifford

From *Myself and I*, by Fannie Stearns Gifford. Reprinted by special arrangement with The Macmillan Company, publishers.

PROVERBS
Proverbs 3:13–17

Happy is the man that findeth wisdom,
And the man that getteth understanding;

For the merchandise of it is better than the merchandise
    of silver;
And the gain thereof than fine gold.

She is more precious than rubies;
And all the things thou canst desire are not to be com-
    pared unto her.

Length of days is in her right hand;
And in her left hand riches and honor.

Her ways are ways of pleasantness;
And all her paths are peace.

—THE BIBLE

HIAWATHA'S FASTING

You shall hear how Hiawatha
Prayed and fasted in the forest,
Not for greater skill in hunting,
Not for greater craft in fishing,
Not for triumphs in the battle,
And renown among the warriors,
But for profit of the people,
For advantage of the nations.

  First he built a lodge for fasting,
Built a wigwam in the forest,
By the shining Big-Sea-Water;
In the blithe and pleasant Spring-time,
In the Moon of Leaves he built it,
And, with dreams and visions many,
Seven whole days and nights he fasted.

  On the first day of his fasting
Through the leafy woods he wandered;
Saw the deer start from the thicket,
Saw the rabbit in his burrow,
Heard the pheasant, Bena, drumming,
Heard the squirrel, Adjidaumo,
Rattling in his hoard of acorns,
Saw the pigeon, the Omeme,
Building nests among the pine trees,
And in flocks the wild goose, Wawa,
Flying to the fen lands northward,

Whirring, wailing far above him.
"Master of Life!" he cried, desponding,
"Must our lives depend on these things?"
  On the next day of his fasting
By the river's brink he wandered,
Through the Muskoday, the meadow,
Saw the wild rice, Mahnomonee,
Saw the blueberry, Meenahga,
And the strawberry, Odahmin,
And the gooseberry, Shahbomin,
And the grapevine, the Bemahgut,
Trailing o'er the alder branches,
Filling all the air with fragrance!
"Master of Life!" he cried, desponding,
"Must our lives depend on these things?"
  On the third day of his fasting
By the lake he sat and pondered,
By the still, transparent water;
Saw the sturgeon, Nahma, leaping,
Scattering drops like beads of wampum,
Saw the yellow perch, the Sahwa,
Like a sunbeam in the water,
Saw the pike, the Maskenozha,
And the herring, Okahahwis,
And the Shawgashee, the crawfish!
"Master of Life!" he cried, desponding,
"Must our lives depend on these things?"

On the fourth day of his fasting
In his lodge he lay exhausted;
From his couch of leaves and branches
Gazing with half-open eyelids,
Full of shadowy dreams and visions,
On the dizzy, swimming landscape,
On the gleaming of the water,
On the splendor of the sunset.

And he saw a youth approaching,
Dressed in garments green and yellow,
Coming through the purple twilight,
Through the splendor of the sunset;
Plumes of green bent o'er his forehead,
And his hair was soft and golden.

Standing at the open doorway,
Long he looked at Hiawatha,
Looked with pity and compassion
On his wasted form and features,
And, in accents like the sighing
Of the South-Wind in the tree-tops,
Said he, "O my Hiawatha!
All your prayers are heard in heaven,
For you pray not like the others;
Not for greater skill in hunting,
Not for greater craft in fishing,
Not for triumph in the battle,
Nor renown among the warriors,

But for profit of the people,
For advantage of the nations.
   "From the Master of Life descending,
I, the friend of man, Mondamin,
Come to warn you and instruct you,
How by struggle and by labor
You shall gain what you have prayed for.
Rise up from your bed of branches,
Rise, O youth, and wrestle with me!"
   Faint with famine, Hiawatha
Started from his bed of branches,
From the twilight of his wigwam
Forth into the flush of sunset
Came, and wrestled with Mondamin;
At his touch he felt new courage
Throbbing in his brain and bosom,
Felt new life and hope and vigor
Run through every nerve and fiber.
   So they wrestled there together
In the glory of the sunset,
And the more they strove and struggled,
Stronger still grew Hiawatha;
Till the darkness fell around them,
And the heron, the Shuh-shuh-gah,
From her nest among the pine trees,
Gave a cry of lamentation,
Gave a scream of pain and famine.

" 'Tis enough!" then said Mondamin,
Smiling upon Hiawatha,
"But tomorrow, when the sun sets,
I will come again to try you."
And he vanished, and was seen not;
Whether sinking as the rain sinks,
Whether rising as the mists rise,
Hiawatha saw not, knew not,
Only saw that he had vanished,
Leaving him alone and fainting,
With the misty lake below him,
And the reeling stars above him.

On the morrow and the next day,
When the sun through heaven descending,
Like a red and burning cinder
From the hearth of the Great Spirit,
Fell into the western waters,
Came Mondamin for the trial,
For the strife with Hiawatha;
Came as silent as the dew comes,
From the empty air appearing,
Into empty air returning,
Taking shape when earth it touches
But invisible to all men
In its coming and its going.

Thrice they wrestled there together
In the glory of the sunset,

Till the darkness fell around them,
Till the heron, the Shuh-shuh-gah,
From her nest among the pine trees,
Uttered her loud cry of famine,
And Mondamin paused to listen.

Tall and beautiful he stood there,
In his garments green and yellow;
To and fro his plumes above him
Waved and nodded with his breathing,
And the sweat of the encounter
Stood like drops of dew upon him.

And he cried, "O Hiawatha!
Bravely have you wrestled with me,
Thrice have wrestled stoutly with me,
And the Master of Life, who sees us,
He will give to you the triumph!"

Then he smiled and said: "Tomorrow
Is the last day of your conflict,
Is the last day of your fasting.
You will conquer and o'ercome me;
Make a bed for me to lie in,
Where the rain may fall upon me,
Where the sun may come and warm me;
Strip these garments, green and yellow,
Strip this nodding plumage from me,
Lay me in the earth and make it
Soft and loose and light above me.

"Let no hand disturb my slumber,
Let no weed nor worm molest me,
Let not Kahgahgee, the raven,
Come to haunt me and molest me,
Only come yourself to watch me,
Till I wake, and start, and quicken,
Till I leap into the sunshine."
And thus saying, he departed;
Peacefully slept Hiawatha,
But he heard the Wawonaissa,
Heard the whippoorwill complaining,
Perched upon his lonely wigwam;
Heard the rushing Sebowisha,
Heard the rivulet rippling near him,
Talking to the darksome forest;
Heard the sighing of the branches,
As they lifted and subsided
At the passing of the night wind,
Heard them, as one hears in slumber
Far-off murmurs, dreamy whispers:
Peacefully slept Hiawatha.
On the morrow came Nokomis,
On the seventh day of his fasting,
Came with food for Hiawatha,
Came imploring and bewailing,
Lest his hunger should o'ercome him,
Lest his fasting should be fatal.

But he tasted not, and touched not,
Only said to her, "Nokomis,
Wait until the sun is setting,
Till the darkness falls around us,
Till the heron, the Shuh-shuh-gah,
Crying from the desolate marshes,
Tells us that the day is ended."
Homeward weeping went Nokomis,
Sorrowing for her Hiawatha,
Fearing lest his strength should fail him,
Lest his fasting should be fatal.
He meanwhile sat weary waiting
For the coming of Mondamin,
Till the shadows, pointing eastward,
Lengthened over field and forest,
Till the sun dropped from the heaven,
Floating on the waters westward,
As a red leaf in the autumn
Falls and floats upon the water,
Falls and sinks into his bosom.
And behold! the young Mondamin,
With his soft and shining tresses,
With his garments green and yellow,
With his long and glossy plumage,
Stood and beckoned at the doorway.
And as one in slumber walking,
Pale and haggard, but undaunted,

From the wigwam Hiawatha
Came and wrestled with Mondamin.

Round about him spun the landscape,
Sky and forest reeled together,
And his strong heart leaped within him,
As the sturgeon leaps and struggles
In a net to break its meshes.
Like a ring of fire around him
Blazed and flared the red horizon,
And a hundred suns seemed looking
At the combat of the wrestlers.

Suddenly upon the greensward
All alone stood Hiawatha,
Panting with his wild exertion,
Palpitating with the struggle;
And before him breathless, lifeless,
Lay the youth, with hair dishevelled,
Plumage torn, and garments tattered,
Dead he lay there in the sunset.

And victorious Hiawatha
Made the grave as he commanded,
Stripped the garments from Mondamin,
Stripped his tattered plumage from him,
Laid him in the earth, and made it
Soft and loose and light above him;
And the heron, the Shuh-shuh-gah,
From the melancholy moorlands,

Gave a cry of lamentation,
Gave a cry of pain and anguish!
   Homeward then went Hiawatha
To the lodge of old Nokomis,
And the seven days of his fasting
Were accomplished and completed.
But the place was not forgotten
Where he wrestled with Mondamin;
Nor forgotten nor neglected
Was the grave where lay Mondamin,
Sleeping in the rain and sunshine,
Where his scattered plumes and garments
Faded in the rain and sunshine.
   Day by day did Hiawatha
Go to wait and watch beside it;
Kept the dark mould soft above it,
Kept it clean from weeds and insects,
Drove away, with scoffs and shoutings,
Kahgahgee, the king of ravens.
   Till at length a small green feather
From the earth shot slowly upward,
Then another and another,
And before the Summer ended
Stood the maize in all its beauty,
With its shining robes about it,
And its long, soft, yellow tresses;
   And in rapture Hiawatha

Cried aloud, "It is Mondamin!
Yes, the friend of man, Mondamin!"
  Then he called to old Nokomis
And Iagoo, the great boaster,
Showed them where the maize was growing,
Told them of his wondrous vision,
Of his wrestling and his triumph,
Of this new gift to the nations,
Which should be their food forever.
  And still later, when the Autumn
Changed the long, green leaves to yellow,
And the soft and juicy kernels
Grew like wampum hard and yellow,
Then the ripened ears he gathered,
Stripped the withered husks from off them,
As he once had stripped the wrestler,
Gave the first Feast of Mondamin,
And made known unto the people
This new gift of the Great Spirit.

— Henry Wadsworth Longfellow

HOW THE POETRY BOOK WAS MADE

The Poetry Book is a series of reading books in nine volumes, one for each year of the elementary and junior high schools. The distinguishing feature of these books is that they are the result of extensive analysis and experimentation to determine the selection and grade placement of poetry material.

The research work for these volumes has been carried out and directed by Miriam Blanton Huber, institute of Educational Research, Teachers College, Columbia University, and Herbert B. Bruner, Bureau of Curriculum Research, Teachers College, Columbia University. They have had the constant help and advice of Charles M. Curry, formerly Professor of Literature, Indiana State Normal School. Every phase of teaching work is represented in the experience of the editors, and all of them have at various times made special studies in the field of children's literature.

The story of the two years spent in the preparation of these books may be briefly summarized as follows:

The first step was to determine the poems which are now generally considered most appropriate for children of the various grades. This was accomplished (1) by considering the subjective opinions of expert teachers of poetry, and (2) by an examination of 900 courses of study and practically all of the most used textbooks, with minute analysis of 30 courses of study and 30 textbooks, in each of grades one to nine. The resulting material formed two-thirds of that subjected to experimentation. From personal choice, previous studies and the opinions of experts in children's reading, additional poems were included, largely from modern poets and material not previously used in textbooks, The experimental material comprised 573 individual poems, increased to almost 900 titles through repetitions arising from the analysis of present practice.

The second step was to subject these poems to the test of use in actual schoolroom and teaching situations. The publishers furnished the material, printed in nine sections. Twelve experimental centers were carefully selected, in order to secure wide geographical distribution and to reach all types of pupils. More than 50,000 children and 1500 teachers were included in the experiment. The method of procedure was such as to secure the most accurate measure of the children's interests in individual poems and to determine in what grade those interests were strongest. Twelve reaction papers were secured from each child and these data were treated statistically. Poems to the number of 535 were given definite grade placement, while 38 poems were not tolerated by children. In the changes in this placement from present practice about as many poems were raised to higher grades as were reduced to lower ones, and about the same number of differences in placement were found from the opinions of experts as from present practice in courses of study and textbooks.

The third step was the making of *The Poetry Book* in nine volumes, based upon the results of this elaborate study and experimentation. Many more poems appear than were used in and placed by the experiment. These additional poems were selected by the editors in the light of the definite interests indicated by the choices of the children. In grade four, for example, 53 titles were placed by the experimental results. One of these poems does not appear in Book 4, and the editors have added 34, making a total of 86 titles in this book. The poems appear in approximately the order in which most teachers will desire to use them. The seasonal interest has been made a basis of arrangement, while poems without this special interest have been distributed in the order of difficulty, or so as to secure variety and balance of subject matter. The ten poems that the experiment indicated as ranking highest in grade four, in order of rank, are as follows:

1. Barbara Frietchie........John Greenleaf Whittier
2. Mr. Nobody..................Author Unknown
3. O Captain! My Captain!........Walt Whitman
4. America the Beautiful......Katharine Lee Bates
5. A Strange Wild Song..............Lewis Carroll
6. The Table and the Chair...........Edward Lear
7. The Height of the Ridiculous
   ....Oliver Wendell Holmes
8. The Flight (The Runaways)....Leroy F. Jackson
9. Book Houses............Annie Fellows Johnston
10. Evening at the Farm. John Townsend Trowbridge

INDEX OF AUTHORS

INDEX OF TITLES